CONTACT USA 1

READING AND VOCABULARY

Paul Abraham
Daphne Mackey

Longman

longman.com

Contact USA 1: Reading and Vocabulary

Pearson Education, 10 Bank Street, White Plains, NY 10606

Executive editor: Laura Le Dréan
Development editors: Debbie Sistino, Tara Maldonado
Production supervisor: Christine Edmonds
Production editor: Christopher Leonowicz
Marketing manager: Joe Chapple
Senior manufacturing buyer: Nancy Flaggman
Cover and interior design: Ann France
Digital layout specialist: Lisa Ghiozzi
Text font: 12/13.5 Minion
Text art: Dave Sullivan

ISBN: 0-13-049623-5

LONGMAN ON THE **WEB**

Longman.com offers online resources for teachers and students. Access our Companion Websites, our online catalog, and our local offices around the world.

Visit us at **longman.com.**

Printed in the United States of America

2 3 4 5 6 7 8 9 10   07 06 05

Contents

To the Teacher

Contact USA 1: Reading and Vocabulary is a text for high-beginning students of English. Although its structure and exercises are aimed primarily at developing academic reading skills and vocabulary, its content is appropriate for all non-native English speakers. The readings provide background information about topics of interest in American culture. The topics were chosen to engage students in both the reading task and subsequent class discussions. The variety of reading types gives students practice with charts, graphs, and first- and third-person narratives. The exercises and discussion questions build students' vocabulary while allowing them to respond to the ideas presented in the text.

Reading

We have written this book on the premise that most students at this level are able to read and understand more in English than they are able to produce. Therefore, although the readings may be challenging for students at this level, the exercises are relatively simple, requiring lower-level reading and vocabulary skills. Students work on the essential reading skills of identifying main ideas and details, reading charts and graphs, making inferences, and using context and multiple encounters to identify and learn vocabulary.

The first reading is a general overview that introduces key vocabulary related to the subject. Reading for Specific Information and A Point of View provide new perspectives on the subject and tie in closely with the speaking activities in each chapter. Students are encouraged to express their ideas about the subject, reinforcing the active use of new vocabulary. Since these readings are often based on opinions and are, as such, debatable, we encourage you to contribute your own personal points of view and to express your own cultural perspectives in any way that might expand your students' knowledge or spark their interests.

Vocabulary

Students learn approximately 200 new words, phrases, and expressions within the context of the readings. An important feature of the *Contact USA* series is the amount of practice students get with new vocabulary. There are at least nine different vocabulary exercises, including guessing from context, application to other contexts, multiple choice, cloze, synonym matching, and even crossword puzzles.

The ability to acquire language through context is an essential component of skilled reading. This book was written in the firm belief that vocabulary can be learned through context if meanings are integrated in the text and the reading level is aligned with the students' language proficiency level. The meaning of much of the vocabulary in *Contact USA 1* is implied within the reading passage, as students soon discover when they complete the first vocabulary exercise, which requires them to analyze words within the context of the reading and compare them to words that they already know. Vocabulary is also recycled throughout the book so that students can recall vocabulary from previous chapters, where it may be used in a different context. The readings make use of language redundancy and elaborated meanings, making constant dictionary use unnecessary. Thus, we encourage you to have students search for meaning within the reading text and through the exercise practice. As shown by vocabulary research, these multiple encounters with vocabulary items lead to acquisition.

Chapter Outline

Units follow this general structure:

A First Look

A. Background Building
B. Reading
C. Topic
D. Vocabulary
E. Reading Comprehension

Look Again

A. Vocabulary
B. Reading Comprehension
C. Reading for Specific Information
D. What Do You Think?

A Point of View

A. Background Building
B. Reading
C. True or False?
D. Vocabulary
E. What Do You Think?

Vocabulary Review

A.   Matching
B.   Sentence Completion
C.   Crossword

The **Teacher's Manual** contains Teaching Guidelines, Vocabulary Review Tests for each chapter, the student book answer key, and three additional readings with comprehension questions.

To the Student

Welcome to *Contact USA 1: Reading and Vocabulary.* This book has two goals:

- to improve your reading ability
- to increase your vocabulary knowledge

In this book, you will read about topics that are interesting to people in general and particularly interesting to people living in the United States. The first reading in every chapter gives general information about the topic. Later in the chapter, you will read charts and graphs with other information about the topic. Finally, you will read someone's opinion—*point of view*—about the topic. If you don't understand the readings at first, try the exercises that follow. They will help you understand the reading.

You will find the vocabulary in the unit used many times, in different exercises and in different readings. Seeing the same words many times will help you learn and remember them. As you know, learning vocabulary is a very important part of learning a language.

In this book, you won't work alone. You will have many opportunities to work with other students, in pairs and in small groups. Working with others and learning from each other is an important part of improving your reading skills and your general English language ability. As you talk about the readings and share your ideas, you will learn to use the new vocabulary in each unit and also improve your speaking.

Acknowledgments

Our thanks to our editors at Pearson Longman ELT: to Laura Le Dréan, who encouraged us to write these lower-level readers; to Dena Daniel for her editorial oversight; and to Debbie Sistino for her outstanding ability as a development editor. We would also like to thank the reviewers of the manuscript:

Abigail Brown, TransPacific Hawaii College, Honolulu, Hawaii; **Adele Camus**, George Mason University, Fairfax, Virginia; **David Dahnke**, North Harris College, Houston, Texas; **Christa Snow**, Nationalities Service Center, Philadelphia, Pennsylvania; **Safineh Tahmassebi**, University of California–Irvine, Irvine, California; **Murat Yesil**, former ESL teacher, Istanbul, Turkey

Biographical Information

Paul Abraham is an Associate Professor of Education and Director of the Master of Arts in Teaching ESL Program at Simmons College, Boston, Massachusetts. He holds a master's in Education in TESL from Boston University and a doctorate in Education from Harvard University in Reading and Language. His interests include reading theory and practice and teacher education.

Daphne Mackey is a lecturer at the English Language Programs, University of Washington, Seattle, Washington. She holds a master's degree in Education from Boston University. She has also taught at the University of Louisville, Boston University, and Pacific Lutheran University. *Contact USA 1* is her eleventh textbook.

Chapter 1 What's Your Name?

A FIRST LOOK

 A BACKGROUND BUILDING

Work with a partner. Discuss these questions.

1. What is your first name? What is your last name (family name)?

2. Look at the pictures on page 2. Who are the people? Are they using first names or last names?

3. Read the list of people in the chart below. What do you call them? Do you use first names or last names? Put a check under *First Name* or *Last Name*. What titles do you use (*Miss, Ms., Mrs., Dr.,* or *Mr.*)? Write the title you use with the last name.

	First Name	Title/Last Name
Your teacher		✓ Ms. Jones
Your classmate		
Your friend's mother		
Your doctor		
Your co-worker		
Your boss		
An older person		

First or Last Name?

1   How do you introduce yourself? Do you use your first
name, your last name, or both? Most people in the United
States use their first and last names when they introduce
themselves. Then, they usually call each other by their first
names. They are not very formal.   5

2   People are usually informal at work. They call their
co-workers by their first names. Many people often call their
bosses by their first names. They also use first names on the
telephone. They say, "Hello, this is Wendy. How can I help you
today?"   10

3   At home, people call their neighbors by their first names.
Sometimes, older people don't like this custom. They don't
want young people to call them by their first names. They don't
think it's polite. So, many parents teach their children to use
titles, such as *Mr.* or *Ms.,* with last names. It is also common   15
for young people to call their teachers and doctors by their
titles and last names.

4   When you use a credit card, a server in a restaurant or a
salesperson in a store may see your name on the card and call
you by your first name. They want to be friendly, but some   20
customers don't like this.

5   With all these different customs, how do you know what to
say? When you're not sure, it's OK to ask, "What do you want
me to call you?"

C TOPIC

Each paragraph in the reading has one main idea, its topic. Read the topics below. Match each topic to a paragraph in the reading. Write the number of the paragraph on the line.

____2____ names people use at work

_____ how to know what name to use

_____ how most people introduce themselves

_____ names servers and salespeople use

_____ what names to use with older people

D VOCABULARY

Look back at the reading to find these words. The line number is in parentheses ( ). Then circle the letter of the word or phrase with a similar meaning.

1. introduce (1)
   a. say, "My name is . . ."   b. say, "Hi"

2. call (4)
   a. use a name   b. ask a question

3. co-workers (7)
   a. people working together   b. people living together

4. neighbors (11)
   a. people you live with   b. people you live near

5. custom (12)
   a. way of thinking   b. way of doing something

6. polite (14)
   a. in a nice way   b. in a quiet way

7. parents (14)
   a. sisters and brothers   b. mothers and fathers

8. common (15)

   a. usual   **b.** not usual

9. friendly (20)

   a. sad   **b.** nice

10. customers (21)

   a. people who sell   **b.** people who buy

E READING COMPREHENSION

Find the answers to the questions in the reading. Underline the answer and write the number of the question next to it.

1. Do most people in the United States use first names or last names?

2. Are people in the United States formal or informal at work?

3. What is the custom some older people don't like?

4. What do young people usually call their teachers?

5. Why do some salespeople use first names?

6. What can you say if you don't know what to call someone?

A VOCABULARY

Complete the questions with words from the box. Then answer the questions with a partner.

boss	formal	polite	titles
customers	introduce	sure	work

1. Do you call everyone at _____ by his or her first name?

2. Do most university students call their professors by their _____ and their last names?

3. At work, do you call your _____ by his or her first name?

4. Do you _____ yourself on the telephone? What do you say?

5. Do you think that it is _____ to call older people by their first names?

6. How can you be _____ about what to call your boss?

7. My grandmother calls all her neighbors *Mr.* or *Mrs.* with their last names. Do you think that's too _____?

8. Do you think salespeople in stores should call _____ by their first names?

B READING COMPREHENSION

Match the phrases in column A with the phrases in column B to make true sentences.

A

B

_____ 1. When people in the United States first introduce themselves, they

a. want to be friendly.

_____ 2. At work, most people

b. use both first and last names.

_____ 3. Some people don't want younger people

c. to call them by their first names.

_____ 4. Sometimes salespeople use first names because they

d. ask them.

_____ 5. When you don't know what to call people, you should

e. are informal and call each other by their first names.

C WHAT DO YOU THINK?

Read the description of the person. In each situation, what would you call the person in English? What would you call each person in your language? Discuss your answers in a small group.

1. George Smith is a doctor. He is 31 years old.

   a. You are 8 years old. George Smith is your doctor.

   b. You are 70 years old. George Smith is your doctor.

   c. You are 25 years old. George Smith is your neighbor.

2. Jennifer Jones is 19 years old. She is a college student. She also teaches dance to young children.

   a. You are 5 years old. Jennifer Jones is your dance teacher.

   b. You are a teacher. Jennifer Jones is your student.

   c. You are a college student. You know Jennifer Jones.

A POINT OF VIEW

A BACKGROUND BUILDING

Discuss the questions in a small group.

1. Do you like your first name? What do you like about it?

2. Does your first name have a special meaning? Does your last name have a special meaning?

3. Are you named after anyone? One of your parents? A grandparent? A friend? Someone famous?

4. Who is the woman in the picture? What is she thinking about?

Here is one person's point of view. Read the story.

My son and his wife are going to have a baby. I'm very excited. I'm going to be a grandmother! There's only one problem—the baby's name. They want to use a name from nature. If it's a girl, her name will be Sunshine. If it's a boy, his name will be Starlight.

I thought they were joking. But they're serious. It's a Native American custom to use names from nature. "OK, fine," I said. "But we're not Native American."

In my family, all the girls are Mary. I'm Mary Jane, and my sister is Mary Ann. I like this custom. I also like the custom of naming a boy after his father and calling him "Junior." My husband is William Smith and my son is William Smith, Jr.

I don't understand young parents today. Why can't they name their children nice, common names? Some parents name their babies after famous people. Some people choose a popular name but spell it differently. For example, they like the name Diana, but they spell it Dianna. What's wrong with Diana?

I like nice, old-fashioned names. If my son and his wife have a girl, I think they should name her after me!

C TRUE OR FALSE?

Read the following sentences carefully. Write T (true) or F (false).

_____ 1. The writer is a grandmother now.

_____ 2. The father wants to name his son Sunshine.

_____ 3. Native American names often come from nature.

_____ 4. The writer is Native American.

_____ 5. The writer's son is William Smith, Jr.

_____ 6. Many young parents today want to give their children unusual names.

_____ 7. The writer likes the way parents name their children today.

_____ 8. The writer wants her granddaughter to be named Mary Ann.

D VOCABULARY

Circle the letter of the word or phrase that best completes each sentence.

1. She's going to France tomorrow. She's very _____ about the trip.
   a. serious   b. excited   c. sure

2. I love the mountains. I go there to enjoy _____.
   a. customs   b. nature   c. work

3. I knew she was _____ about the problem when she started to laugh.
   a. joking   b. calling   c. working

4. Don't laugh! I'm _____ about this.
   a. polite   b. sure   c. serious

5. She is a _____ author. I read three of her books.
   a. formal   b. famous   c. polite

6. You need to _____ the best answer.
   a. try   b. choose   c. spell

7. A lot of boys are named Michael. It's a _____ name.

   a. friendly   **b.** family   **c.** popular

8. How do you _____ your name? Does it start with an *f* or *ph*?

   a. spell   **b.** show   **c.** call

E ▶ WHAT DO YOU THINK?

Discuss the questions in a small group.

1. The woman in the reading told her son and daughter-in-law that she didn't like the names for her new grandchild. Was this a good thing to do?

2. Do fathers and sons ever have the same first name in your language? Do mothers and daughters? How do you show the difference?

3. A family has seven children. The parents gave each child a name beginning with the letter *R*. The children were Ronald, Rhonda, Richard, Rose, and so on. What do you think about this?

4. A woman was named Karen. She never liked her name. When she was 18, she changed her name to Kristyra. What do you think about this?

5. In the United States, there are some names that are for both girls and boys. Is this true in other countries?

F ▶ READING FOR SPECIFIC INFORMATION

Read the stories and answer the questions. Discuss your answers in groups.

Coincidences

Story 1

Once, there were three people on a long train ride. They introduced themselves. One was named John. Another was named Philip. The third was named John Philip. It was a coincidence.

Story 2

Twin brothers were separated at birth. They went to live with different families. Each family named the baby boy James. When the two boys grew up, each married a woman named Linda. They each had a son. One brother named his son James Alan. The other brother named his son James Allen. And they both had dogs named Toy.

Story 3

Patel is an unusual name in the United States. Two girls named Sheena Patel went to the same college in the same year. They met each other, and they became friends. One girl came from California. The other came from Kentucky. They told their families about the coincidence. But that wasn't the only coincidence. Both fathers were doctors. Both fathers were born in the same city. Not only that—the fathers were roommates at college!

1. What is a coincidence?

2. What are the names of the three people in Story 1?

3. How many coincidences are there in Story 2? What are they?

4. How many coincidences are there in Story 3? What are they?

5. Which of the coincidences do you think was the most unusual?

6. Do you know anyone who has the same first name as you do? The same last name? The same first *and* last name?

VOCABULARY REVIEW

A ▸ MATCHING

Match each word to the word or phrase with a similar meaning.

_____ 1. customers   **a.** nice

_____ 2. friendly   **b.** usual

_____ 3. serious   **c.** at the beginning

_____ 4. common   **d.** people who have children

_____ 5. formal   **e.** person who tells other people what to do at work

_____ 6. boss   **f.** people who come to a store to buy something

_____ 7. first   **g.** not funny

_____ 8. parents   **h.** very polite

B ▸ SENTENCE COMPLETION

Complete the sentences with words from the box.

call	customers	friendly	named after	sure
choose	excited	introduce	polite	work

1. Are you going to _____ the baby Joseph or Joe?

2. I was _____ my grandfather. His name was Patrick also.

3. She always goes to that store to buy food. She's one of their best _____.

4. He never says hello or smiles. I don't think he's very _____.

5. Is it _____ to call a teacher by her first name?

6. I think I know the answer, but I'm not _____. Is it *B?*

7. Our children got a new dog. They are very _____.

8. I start _____ at 8:30 and I end at 4:30.

9. I don't know his name. He didn't _____ himself.

10. They can't decide what to call the baby. It's not easy to

    _____ a name.

C CROSSWORD

Complete the puzzle.

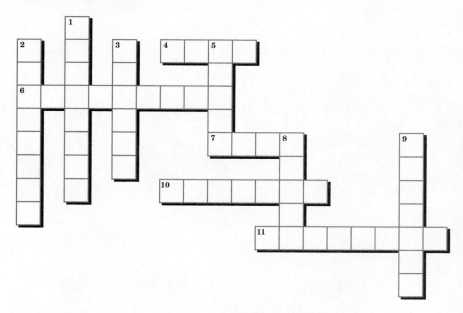

Across

4. a person who tells other people what to do at work

6. tell one person's name to another person

7. not first

10. people who have children

11. someone who lives near you

Down

1. person shopping in a store

2. nice to people

3. make a decision

5. "You _____ it E I G H T, not A T E."

8. Dr., Mr., Ms.

9. not funny

Chapter 2 Meeting People

1. _____

2. _____

3. _____

4. _____

5. _____

6. _____

7. _____

8. _____

bus	gym	religious place	supermarket
coffee shop	online	school	work

A FIRST LOOK

A BACKGROUND BUILDING

Work with a partner. Discuss these questions.

1. Look at the pictures on page 16. Match the words to the pictures.

2. Which of these are good places to meet new friends?

   _____

3. Where did you meet:

   Your best friend? _____

   Your husband/wife or girlfriend/boyfriend? _____

4. Where did your parents meet? _____

5. Which of the places on page 16 are good places to meet someone special?

   _____

B READING

Meeting People

1   Where is the best place to meet people? First, it's a place
   where the same people spend a lot of time. Maybe that's why
   it's easy for children to make new friends in their
   neighborhoods and at school. They see the same people there
   every day.   5

2 Second, there needs to be time for people to talk. Adults meet a lot of people at work or at school, but how many become friends? One problem is that they don't have time to talk. To become friends, people need time to get to know each other. 10

3 That's why it's harder for new people to make new friends. For example, when a teenager goes to a new school, the kids there already have groups of friends. They don't always have time for new friends and are not always friendly to a new student. 15

4 How do people meet someone special? Many years ago, parents chose partners for their sons and daughters. Parents sometimes paid a *matchmaker* to help. The matchmaker knew a lot of people and introduced the families to each other.

5 Things are different now. Most young people don't want 20 their parents or a matchmaker to choose a partner for them. They want to meet people on their own.

6 What happens when people don't meet anyone special? Some people pay a company to introduce them to partners. This can be expensive, but many people think it's a good idea. 25 They are busy with their jobs and don't have time to meet people on their own.

7 It is also possible to "meet" people online. Some people meet in chat rooms. Other people pay matchmaking companies to help them meet people. One company says that 30 it had more than 1,000 weddings in six years.

8 If you want to meet someone special, remember how people make friends. Go to places where you see the same people and have time to talk. Don't worry. Smile and start to talk to someone. 35

C TOPIC

Read the topics below. Match each topic to a paragraph in the reading. Write the number of the paragraph on the line.

_____ people need time to talk to make friends

_____ using matchmakers many years ago

_____ where you can meet people

_____ meeting people online

_____ things to do to meet someone special

_____ using companies to find someone special

_____ what young people want now

_____ making friends is hard for new people

D VOCABULARY

Look back at the reading to find these words. The line number is in parentheses ( ). Then circle the letter of the word or phrase with a similar meaning.

1. neighborhood (4)
   a. place where you live
   b. place where you eat

2. adults (6)
   a. parents
   b. people 18 and older

3. problem (8)
   a. question
   b. difficult thing

4. teenager (12)
   a. 10–13 years old
   b. 13–19 years old

5. partners (17)
   a. husbands or wives
   b. parents

6. on their own (22)
    a. by themselves   **b.** with someone else

7. weddings (31)
    a. marriages   **b.** meetings

8. worry (34)
    a. feel unhappy   **b.** feel sick

E READING COMPREHENSION

Find the answers to the questions in the reading. Underline the answer and write the number of the question next to it.

1. Where is the best place to meet new people?

2. Why is it easy for children to make new friends?

3. In the past, people used a matchmaker. What was a matchmaker's job?

4. What are two ways of meeting that young people use today?

5. Which is the better place to meet new people? Why?
    a. in a Spanish class or in a restaurant
    b. waiting for a class to start or waiting for a movie to start
    c. at a doctor's office or at a supermarket

LOOK AGAIN

A VOCABULARY

Circle the letter of the word or phrase closest in meaning to the boldfaced word(s) in the sentence.

1. She **spends** a lot of **time** studying. She gets really good grades.
   a. uses time   b. gives time   c. pays for time

2. He doesn't speak English, so it was **harder** for him to meet people.
   a. easier   b. not as easy   c. faster

3. She met **someone special**, and now they are getting married.
   a. a good friend   b. a matchmaker   c. a possible partner

4. I want to **get to know** my new neighbors. They seem very nice.
   a. talk to   b. meet   c. call

5. They **paid** the matchmaker **a lot of money** for her work.
   a. got money from   b. bought   c. gave money to

6. They started an online matchmaking **company**. She is the president, and he fixes the computers.
   a. group   b. business   c. family

7. We are going to have a small wedding. Big weddings are too **expensive**.
   a. cost a lot of money   b. have a lot of people   c. have a lot of food

8. We always have a nice **chat** when we see each other.
   a. time   b. talk   c. meal

B ▸ READING COMPREHENSION

Circle the letter of the answer that best completes each sentence. Look back at the reading to find the answers.

1. It is probably easier for _____ to make new friends.
   a. a 6-year-old
   b. a teenager

2. Adults usually _____ a lot of people.
   a. meet
   b. become friends with

3. People are sometimes not friendly to new people because they have _____.
   a. no time
   b. a lot of time

4. A coffee shop you go to _____ is a good place to meet people.
   a. one time
   b. every morning

5. Nowadays, parents _____ choose their children's husbands and wives.
   a. usually
   b. don't

6. A matchmaker's job is to _____ people to each other.
   a. introduce
   b. talk about

7. Online matchmaking _____ people find partners.
   a. helps
   b. doesn't help

8. If you want to meet new friends, you should be _____.
   a. friendly
   b. worried

READING FOR SPECIFIC INFORMATION

The chart shows places where most people meet possible partners. Look at the chart and answer the questions.

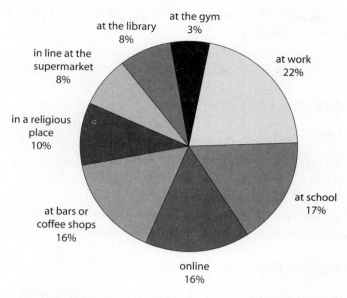

at the gym
3%

at the library
8%

in line at the
supermarket
8%

in a religious
place
10%

at work
22%

at school
17%

at bars or
coffee shops
16%

online
16%

SOURCE: John Fetto, "What a Girl (and Boy) Wants." *American Demographics,* 23, no. 4 (April 2001), p. 10–11.

1. What place on the chart is most common?

   _____

2. What place on the chart is the least common?

   _____

3. Do more people meet at coffee shops or online?

   _____

4. Do more people meet at the library or at the supermarket?

   _____

5. Do more people meet at the gym or in a religious place?

_____

6. Look at your answer to item 5 on page 17. Are your choices the same as the ones in the chart?

_____

◆D▶ WHAT DO YOU THINK?

Discuss the questions in a small group.

1. Is it more difficult for children, teenagers, or adults to make friends? Why?

2. Where do you see the most people and also have time to talk? If you were not a student, where could you meet people?

3. What surprised you about the chart on page 23? Why?

4. What other places do you think should be on the chart? Where else do people meet?

A POINT OF VIEW

A ◢ BACKGROUND BUILDING

Look at the picture and discuss the questions in a small group.

1. What is this Web page for?

2. Is this a good way to meet someone special?

Here is one person's point of view. Read the story.

I have two daughters. One is married and has three young children. My other daughter is 29 and still single. She had a boyfriend, but they broke up two years ago. I know that she wants to get married and have children of her own, so I was sorry when she and her boyfriend didn't get married.

Now, I'm worried. Last week she decided to use a dating service. This company will match her with a man. Then they'll go out on dates and see if they like each other. I think this is a terrible way to meet people. It's not safe. Also, she can't tell people, "We met through a dating service!"

Oh well . . . it's not as bad as my friend Martha's daughter. She's using an online company to meet people. Now, that's really not safe! A man can lie online. He can say he is the perfect man for her. But is he really? How can she know?

I'd like to go back to the old days. Well, I don't want to choose my daughter's husband, but I don't like dating services or this online matchmaking! In the old days, matchmakers knew people's families. They knew that the people were good people from good families. That was a better way to meet people.

C ▸ TRUE OR FALSE?

Read the following sentences carefully. Write T (true) or F (false).

_____ 1. The writer is probably a woman.

_____ 2. The married daughter is 29.

_____ 3. The writer is worried about both daughters.

_____ 4. The writer didn't like the daughter's boyfriend.

_____ 5. The writer's daughter is using an online dating company.

_____ 6. The writer is unhappy about the dating company idea.

_____ 7. The writer's friend is named Martha.

_____ 8. The writer thinks that men will always tell the truth online.

_____ 9. The writer wants to choose a husband for the daughter.

_____ 10. In the old days, matchmakers knew more information about the people they were matching.

D ▸ VOCABULARY

Part 1

Circle the letter of the word or phrase closest in meaning to the boldfaced word(s) in the sentence.

1. **I'm sorry** that you can't come to the party.
   a. I feel bad   **b.** I don't care

2. You should meet her. She's **single** and very nice.
   a. unusual   **b.** not married

3. She was not happy with her boyfriend. **She broke up with him**.
   a. He is still her boyfriend.   **b.** He is not her boyfriend now.

4. She had a green dress, but it was hard to find shoes to **match**.
   a. go together   **b.** buy

5. That's a **terrible** idea! I don't want to go to that restaurant.

   a. very good   **b.** very bad

6. Many older people **lie** about their age. They want to seem younger.

   a. say something false   **b.** be happy

7. It was a **perfect** day. It was warm and sunny.

   a. famous   **b.** just right

8. Our neighborhood is very **safe**. My children walk home from school by themselves every day.

   a. nice   **b.** not dangerous

Part 2

Complete the paragraphs with words from the box.

coffee shop	married	online	safe	wife
go on a date	matchmakers	partners	special	work

    I know a lot of people who can't meet someone _____
 1
in the usual ways, at school or at _____. Some people are
 2
using dating services. These services help people meet possible

_____. They are like _____ from the past.
 3   4
Other people meet _____. Some people say that meeting
 5
this way is not _____. I don't agree. But if you meet
 6
someone online, you should also plan to _____ to a
 7
restaurant or a(n) _____, a place where there are a lot
 8
of people.

Online meeting works for a lot of people. I have a friend who met his

_____ a few years ago online. Now they are

9

_____ and have two children.

10

E WHAT DO YOU THINK?

Check the sentences you agree with. Then discuss your answers in a small group.

_____ 1. It's a good idea for parents to choose their children's husbands or wives.

_____ 2. Matchmaking is sometimes a good idea.

_____ 3. I would pay money to meet someone special.

_____ 4. It's not safe to meet someone online.

_____ 5. There are a lot of places to meet people, so you don't need to use a matchmaking company.

_____ 6. An online matchmaking company is not as good as a regular matchmaking company.

_____ 7. Most people lie when they introduce themselves online.

_____ 8. It's important to know someone's family before you decide to get married.

VOCABULARY REVIEW

A MATCHING

Match each word to the word or phrase with a similar meaning.

_____ 1. wedding   **a.** not an adult

_____ 2. company   **b.** wife or husband

_____ 3. perfect   **c.** when people get married

_____ 4. single   **d.** feel bad about something

_____ 5. meet   **e.** exactly right

_____ 6. be sorry   **f.** place where people work

_____ 7. teenager   **g.** not married

_____ 8. partner   **h.** get to know

B SENTENCE COMPLETION

Complete the sentences with words from the box.

broke up	expensive	pay	special
chat	neighborhood	sorry	spend time

1. She lives in my _____, so I see her every day.

2. I don't go to that restaurant because it's too _____.

3. We never see each other. Let's _____ together tonight.

4. I just wanted to talk to you, so I called to _____.

5. They aren't getting married now. They _____.

6. I'm _____ to hear about your problem.

7. I like to go to the movies, but I don't like to _____ a lot to see them.

8. He really wants to meet someone _____ and get married.

C ▸ CROSSWORD

Complete the puzzle.

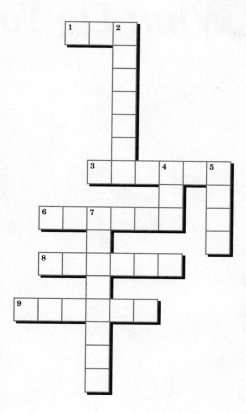

Across

1. a place to exercise
3. not children
6. not today, but maybe tomorrow or another day in the _____
8. more difficult
9. on the Internet

Down

2. not single
4. not tell the truth
5. not dangerous
7. very bad

Chapter 3

What Do You Do?

a.

b.

c.

d.

e.

f.

g.

h.

i.

j.

A FIRST LOOK

 A BACKGROUND BUILDING

Work with a partner. Discuss these questions.

1. Look at the pictures on page 32.

    a. Match the jobs below to the pictures. Write the letter of the picture next to the job.

    b. What do people with these jobs do? Draw a line from the job to the phrase that describes what the person does.

__d__	an auto mechanic	cuts and styles hair
_____	a firefighter	helps customers in a bank
_____	a bank teller	drives a bus
_____	a bus driver	prepares food
_____	a child-care worker	takes care of people's teeth
_____	a hairdresser	puts out fires
_____	a cook	fixes cars
_____	a dentist	works in an office
_____	a plumber	takes care of children
_____	an administrative assistant	fixes water pipes

2. What kind of training do you need to do these jobs? Do you need a college education? Do you need to go to a special technical school? Can you learn "on-the-job"?

3. Can you guess which job pays the highest salary in the United States? Which job pays the lowest salary?

4. Would you like to have any of these jobs? Why or why not?

What Do You Do?

1   "What do you do?" This is a question people in the United
States often ask when they first meet. Of course, it means,
"What kind of work do you do?" People ask about our jobs
because they want to know if they have something in common
with us. They also want to know if we have an interesting or   5
important job.

2   We are always thinking about work. Even children think
about what kind of work they will do. Adults often ask them,
"What do you want to be when you grow up?" Children have
great plans. They say, "I want to be the president." Or "I want   10
to be a famous singer."

3   Most children will never be the president or a famous
singer. They have to find a job that is right for them and that
uses their skills. A job as a salesperson might be good for a
very friendly person. A job as an office worker might not be a   15
good match for someone who likes to be outside. It's
important to be realistic and to use our abilities in our work.

4   Work is very important. Most people spend about forty
hours per week at work. That's one-third of each day. It's
important to have a job that is interesting. It's also important to   20
have a job that we like to do.

5   Don't worry if you don't have the perfect job. People in the
United States change their jobs five times during their lives.
So, if you don't have the right job today, maybe your next job
will be better.   25

C TOPIC

Read the topics below. Match each topic to a paragraph in the reading. Write the number of the paragraph on the line.

_____ children think about work

_____ people change jobs often

_____ we spend a lot of time at work

_____ people ask about work

_____ find a job that is a good match

D VOCABULARY

Look back at the reading to find these words. The line number is in parentheses ( ). Then circle the letter of the word or phrase with a similar meaning.

1. have something in common with (4)
   a. have the same interests
   b. have different interests

2. adults (8)
   a. grown-ups
   b. children

3. plans (10)
   a. what you will do
   b. what you will need

4. right (13)
   a. good
   b. easy

5. skills (14)
   a. special tools
   b. special knowledge

6. outside (16)
   a. not in a building
   b. in a building

7. to be realistic (17)
   a. to think something is fun
   b. to think something is possible

8. abilities (17)

    a. things you can do   **b.** things you want to do

9. worry (22)

    a. feel nervous   **b.** feel sick

10. perfect (22)

    a. the best for you   **b.** the first for you

 E READING COMPREHENSION

Find the answers to the questions in the reading. Underline the answer and write the number of the question next to it.

1. Why do people ask, "What do you do?"

2. What kind of job plans do many children have?

3. What is an example of a good job for a friendly person?

4. What is an example of a bad job for someone who likes to be outside?

5. According to this reading, you don't need to worry if you don't have the perfect job. Why?

A VOCABULARY

Complete the paragraphs with words from the box.

famous	in common with	perfect	realistic
important	match	plans	skills

What do professional baseball, football, and basketball players have

_____ actors? One thing is high salaries. When athletes or

1

actors become _____, they can make a lot of money. Most

2

athletes and actors have very good _____, but some people

3

think their salaries are too high. They don't think the salaries are a good

_____ for the job.

4

Children often have _____ to be a famous actor or

5

football player. But, of course, all children will not become famous. We

all want to have the _____ job. But, it's _____

6 7

for all of us to be _____ about what we can and cannot do.

8

B READING COMPREHENSION

Circle the letter of the answer that best completes each sentence. Look back at the reading to find the answers.

1. Another way to ask "What kind of work do you do?" is _____.

   a. "What do you do?"   **b.** "How do you do?"

2. People ask about our jobs because they want to know if we _____.

   a. are good workers   **b.** have something in common with them

3. Even children think about work because people _____.

   a. have great plans   **b.** ask them about the future

4. Becoming a famous singer is an example of _____.

   a. a great plan   **b.** an adult

5. If someone is friendly, then a job as a salesperson _____.

   a. uses the person's skills   **b.** isn't a good match

6. We need to find interesting jobs because we _____.

   a. can use our abilities   **b.** spend a lot of time at work

7. Most people spend _____ a day at work.

   a. eight hours   **b.** forty hours

8. If you do not like the job you have now, don't worry. You will probably _____ in the future.

   a. change jobs   **b.** enjoy this job

READING FOR SPECIFIC INFORMATION

This chart shows the average salaries for a few jobs in the United States in 2002. These salaries are for people who are just starting in these jobs. They do not have a lot of experience. Read the information in the chart. Then discuss the questions with a partner.

Jobs and Salaries			
Administrative assistant	$26,615	General laborer	$23,810
Auto mechanic	$28,822	Hairdresser	$19,786
Bank teller	$20,226	Janitor	$21,412
Bicycle repair person	$18,221	Machine operator	$23,628
Bus driver	$16,047	Plumber	$29,089
Child-care worker	$19,547	Police officer	$41,450
Cook	$29,428	Teacher	$43,239
Dentist	$63,288	Telemarketer	$23,442
Firefighter	$34,723	Web designer	$44,202

SOURCE: http://www.salaries.com

1. Who has the highest salary?

2. Who has the lowest salary?

3. Find jobs that have about the same salary.

   a. _____ and _____

   b. _____ and _____

D ▶ WHAT DO YOU THINK?

Discuss the questions in a small group.

1. What salary on the chart surprised you? Was it high or low?

2. Were you correct in your guesses about the highest and lowest salaries for the jobs listed on page 33?

3. Thirty years ago, baseball players earned less than $40,000 per year. Today the average salary is over $2 million per year. What do you think about this? Is the salary a good match for the job? Why or why not?

4. When you were a child, what job did you want to have?

5. The reading on page 34 says people should "find a job that is right for them and that uses their skills." Do you think this is always possible? Why or why not?

6. The reading also says that people change jobs five times in their lives. Do you think this will be true for you?

A BACKGROUND BUILDING

Look at the picture and discuss the questions in a small group.

1. What is this man's job?

2. How does he feel about it?

Here is one person's point of view. Read the story.

I need to make a decision soon about my future. I hate making decisions! This one is about my job. I went to college and got my degree in business. Now I have a job as a bank teller. My parents think this is wonderful. They're proud of me. They talk about me to their friends. They think banking is an important job.

I think working in a bank is boring. I really love cars, and I'd like to be a mechanic. My parents, however, think that is a terrible idea. They say that I won't make any money. I'll be busy all the time. I'll be dirty all the time. I don't care about status, what other people think of my job. I'd rather be dirty and happy than clean and bored. I also don't think people in banks make much money. Only people with important jobs have high salaries. I don't really care about money, either. When I fix a car, I feel good about it. I don't really feel very good about anything I do at the bank.

So I asked my parents, "What's more important—being happy or having a job that everyone thinks is important?" They said that a high-status job will help me be happy in other ways. I'll meet nice girls and be able to marry one of them. I'll have a job my children can be proud of. I don't get it. I think being an auto mechanic is a good job. Maybe I'll be able to have my own shop some day. That would make me proud.

C TRUE OR FALSE?

Read the following sentences carefully. Write T (true) or F (false).

_____ 1. It's easy for this person to make decisions.

_____ 2. The writer thinks being a bank teller is a boring job.

_____ 3. The writer has a college degree.

_____ 4. The writer's parents think that being a bank teller is a more important job than being an auto mechanic.

_____ 5. The writer's dream is to have an auto repair shop.

_____ 6. People who have important jobs in the bank make a lot of money.

_____ 7. Making a lot of money is important to the writer.

_____ 8. Other people's ideas are important to the writer.

D VOCABULARY

Circle the letter of the word or phrase closest in meaning to the boldfaced word(s) in the sentence.

Part 1

1. It's very hard to **make a decision**. I don't know what to do.
   a. choose   **b.** get a job   **c.** change

2. My parents **care about** what other people think, but I don't.
   a. forget about   **b.** think it's important   **c.** spend time on

3. That's a **wonderful** idea, but it will cost a lot.
   a. very good   **b.** possible   **c.** OK

4. My parents are **proud of** me because I worked hard and got good grades.
   a. feel good about   **b.** unhappy with   **c.** talk about

5. This job is **boring**, but it pays well.

   a. difficult   **b.** important   **c.** not interesting

6. I like my job; **however**, I want to earn a higher salary.

   a. but   **b.** now   **c.** and

7. **High status** isn't important to me. I don't care what people think.

   a. A good feeling   **b.** An important level   **c.** A good salary

8. **I'd rather be happy than rich.**

   a. I want to be happy.   **b.** I want to be rich.   **c.** I want to be happy and rich.

9. That's a funny story. Don't you **get it**?

   a. read it   **b.** buy it   **c.** understand it

10. My sister and I sleep in the same room now, but soon I'll have **my own** room.

   a. belonging to me and my sister   **b.** belonging to me   **c.** belonging to my sister

Part 2

Complete the sentences with words from the box.

bored	dirty	however	make a decision	proud of
clean	get it	I'd rather	own	shop

1. He is trying to _____ about what college to go to.

2. She likes her work; _____, she doesn't make a lot of money. She'll never be rich.

3. _____ be happy than rich.

4. My job is really interesting. I am never _____ at work.

5. I think calculus is difficult. I just don't _____.

6. I'm _____ my brother. He just became a dentist.

7. I was working in the garden all day. I'm really _____.
I need to take a shower.

8. I left my car in the _____. The auto mechanic needs to
fix it.

9. Put on a(n) _____ shirt. We're going out to dinner.

10. You don't have to give him any paper. He has his _____
notebook.

E ▸ WHAT DO YOU THINK?

**Check the sentences you agree with. Then discuss your answers
in a small group.**

_____ 1. The writer should stay at the bank.

_____ 2. The writer should leave the bank.

_____ 3. The writer should become an auto mechanic.

_____ 4. An interesting job is more important than a job other people
think is good.

_____ 5. A high salary is the most important thing in a job.

_____ 6. It's important to have a job that people think is important.

VOCABULARY REVIEW

A MATCHING

Match each word to the word or phrase with a similar meaning.

_____ 1. adults   **a.** great, very good

_____ 2. right   **b.** not inside

_____ 3. in common with **c.** not clean

_____ 4. perfect   **d.** correct

_____ 5. boring   **e.** grown-ups

_____ 6. dirty   **f.** exactly right

_____ 7. outside   **g.** not interesting

_____ 8. wonderful   **h.** similar to

B SENTENCE COMPLETION

Complete the sentences with words from the box.

in common with	match	plans	realistic
make a decision	own	plumber	salary

1. I wanted to be a doctor, but that wasn't a(n) _____ idea. I wasn't a good student.

2. I use my sister's cell phone, but I'd like to have my _____ phone.

3. He's a nice person, but I have nothing _____ him. We never have anything to talk about.

4. I need to _____ about which job to choose.

5. It's an interesting job, but it doesn't pay well. I need to have a higher _____ so I can pay my bills.

6. The water is coming out onto the floor of the bathroom. Quick! Call the _____!

7. She likes to go to parties and talk to people. He likes to stay home and read. They don't seem like a good _____.

8. Do you have any _____ for the weekend?

C CROSSWORD

Complete the puzzle.

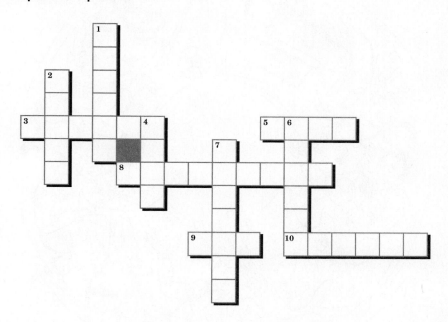

Across

3. well-known
5. "I don't ___ about money."
8. great
9. "What do you mean? I don't ____ it."
10. special abilities

Down

1. "We're similar. We have a lot in ____."
2. ideas for the future
4. small store
6. not children
7. exactly right

Chapter 4 Stressed Out

A **BACKGROUND BUILDING**

Complete the survey and answer the questions.

1. Read the following items. How often is this true for you? Circle a number to show how often. Then add up your total score.

    1 = never true   **5** = usually true

    a. I feel tired.   1 2 3 4 5

    b. I feel sad.   1 2 3 4 5

    c. I forget things.   1 2 3 4 5

    d. I am often in a bad mood.   1 2 3 4 5

    e. I don't want to talk to people.   1 2 3 4 5

    f. I have trouble sleeping.   1 2 3 4 5

    g. I get sick a lot.   1 2 3 4 5

    h. I'm not doing well in my work or study.   1 2 3 4 5

    i. I don't like going to work or school.   1 2 3 4 5

    j. I'm not interested in many things.   1 2 3 4 5

                                                    Total _____

If your total is:	
10–20	You are doing well.
21–30	You are OK.
31–40	You are stressed.
41–50	You are very stressed.

2. Share your score with a partner. If you had a high score, you are probably stressed out. Why do you think you are stressed out?

3. Look at the picture on page 48. Why is the woman stressed out?

B READING

Stressed Out?

1   Are you working too much? Do you feel stressed? You're
not alone. Fifty-seven percent of workers in the United States
say that they are stressed out. Thirty-eight percent of these
people say that they have health problems because of stress.

2   Stress is when you feel worried about too many things. At   5
first it's mental, in your head. Then it becomes physical. Your
body starts to feel bad, too. When you feel stress, you may get
headaches or have stomach problems. People with stress
often have trouble sleeping and get sick more often.
Sometimes it's hard to think clearly. It's hard to finish   10
your work.

3   What can you do if you feel stressed? The first step is to
ask, "Why am I stressed out? What situations are causing me
too much stress? Am I in control of these situations? Can I
change them?" Everyone has some stress, and some stress is   15
good for you. It makes life interesting and helps you
experience new things. However, some situations cause *too
much* stress.

4   The next step is to learn how to understand stress. You will
always have stress in your life, so it's important to figure out   20
what you can do to manage stress.

SOURCE: Kathianne M. Kowalski, "Coping with Stress." *Current Health 2*, 27, no. 1 (September 2000), p. 6.
© 2000 Weekly Reader Corp.

C TOPIC

Read the topics below. Match each topic to a paragraph in the reading. Write the number of the paragraph on the line.

_____ what stress is

_____ learn how to understand stress

_____ many people feel stress

_____ questions about what makes you stressed

D VOCABULARY

Look back at the reading to find these words. The line number is in parentheses ( ). Then circle the letter of the word or phrase with a similar meaning.

1. alone (2)
   a. with other people

   b. not with other people

2. mental (6)
   a. of the mind

   b. of the body

3. physical (6)
   a. of the mind

   b. of the body

4. have trouble (9)
   a. have a problem

   b. be in a bad situation

5. hard (10)
   a. difficult

   b. different

6. clearly (10)
   a. well

   b. slowly

7. in control (14)
   a. able to understand

   b. able to make a decision about

8. cause (17)

    a. make something happen   **b.** show something

9. figure out (20)

    a. do   **b.** understand

10. manage (21)

    a. take care of   **b.** find

E ▸ READING COMPREHENSION

Find the answers to the questions in the reading. Underline the answer and write the number of the question next to it.

1. How many workers in the United States feel stressed out?

2. What percentage of people have health problems because of stress?

3. What kinds of stress does the reading discuss?

4. What can happen when you feel stress?

5. What should you do if you are stressed?

6. Why do we have to learn how to manage stress?

LOOK AGAIN

A VOCABULARY

Complete the paragraphs with words from the box.

causes	in control	physical	step
feel	manage	situations	worry

Do you sometimes _____ stressed out? Everyone is in

1

stressful _____ sometimes. There are many

2

_____ of stress: work, family, money. We often

3

_____ about these things. We feel stress when we are not

4

_____. For example, your boss says that he wants a project

5

on Monday morning, and you know that you don't have time to get it

done.

The signs of stress can be mental or _____. What can

6

we do about stress? The first _____ is to understand where

7

the stress comes from. Sometimes, it is helpful just to know why you are

stressed. It is also important to know how to _____ stress.

8

Everyone has different ways of managing stress. What works best for you?

Circle the letter of the answer that best completes each sentence. Look back at the reading to find the answers.

1. Most people in the United States say that _____ stress.

   a. they never have   **b.** they feel   **c.** they enjoy

2. _____ percent of U.S. workers say that they are stressed out.

   a. Fifty-seven   **b.** Thirty-eight   **c.** Seventy-five

3. If you are stressed, you _____.

   a. are alone   **b.** are similar to many people   **c.** have health problems

4. Stress _____ causes headaches and stomach problems.

   a. always   **b.** sometimes   **c.** never

5. Stress _____ mental and physical.

   a. is both   **b.** may be both   **c.** is never

6. The reading says that the first step in feeling better is to _____ what causes you stress.

   a. figure out   **b.** stop   **c.** change

7. You _____ control everything that causes stress.

   a. can   **b.** can't   **c.** need to

8. The writer thinks that some stress _____.

   a. is easy to manage   **b.** is very unusual   **c.** is good

C WHAT DO YOU THINK?

Discuss the questions in a small group.

1. What situations cause you stress?

2. When you are stressed, how do you feel?

3. What can you do about stress?

A POINT OF VIEW

A BACKGROUND BUILDING

Discuss the questions in a small group.

1. How old is the person in the picture?

2. What are some of the things she is worried about?

3. Adults feel more stress than teenagers. Do you agree or disagree? Why?

B ▸ READING

Here is one person's point of view. Read the story.

Everyone thinks that grown-ups are the only ones with big problems. I disagree! My name is Lee. I'm a teenager, and I have a lot of things to worry about. I'm in our school play, so I have to practice four nights a week. I'm also in an advanced class at school, so I have a ton of homework. As a matter of fact, I have two projects due on the same day this week. Now, on top of everything else, I have a cold.

My mom expects me to get good grades so I can get into a good college. She thinks I can handle everything, including my chores. Last night after dinner, she asked me to do the dishes, and then she got really mad at me when I said I didn't have time. Well, OK, I didn't actually say I didn't have time. I yelled, "Why is it my job to do the dishes? It's not fair! I don't have time!" My mom was mad at me, but it isn't fair. I don't have time! I have too much to do!

C ▸ TRUE OR FALSE?

Read the following sentences carefully. Write T (true) or F (false).

_____ 1. Lee is in her 20s.

_____ 2. Lee has a lot of things to worry about.

_____ 3. Lee is not feeling sick.

_____ 4. Her mother wants her to go to a good college.

_____ 5. We know that Lee gets good grades.

_____ 6. Lee doesn't have much homework.

_____ 7. Lee earns money by washing the dishes.

_____ 8. Lee has enough time to do her homework.

Circle the letter of the word or phrase closest in meaning to the boldfaced word(s) in the sentence.

1. **Grown-ups** think they're the only ones with problems.

   a. Teenagers   **b.** Children   **c.** Adults

2. We have to read ten pages in the book. **On top of** that, we have to practice for the play.

   a. Before   **b.** After   **c.** In addition to

3. What kind of **project** do you have to do?

   a. example   **b.** special work   **c.** job

4. The homework **is due** tomorrow.

   a. must be finished   **b.** is going to be late   **c.** is very hard

5. Everyone **expected** Sue would marry Bob, but she married his friend Joe.

   a. knew   **b.** believed   **c.** disagreed

6. I have a lot to do, but I can **handle** everything.

   a. touch   **b.** find   **c.** take care of

7. I clean my house once a week. What **chores** do you have to do?

   a. regular jobs   **b.** special work   **c.** part-time work

8. My friend **got mad at** me because I didn't call her.

   a. got angry with   **b.** understood   **c.** worried about

9. Everyone **yelled** "Surprise!" when they walked into the room.

   a. said   **b.** shouted   **c.** heard

10. It doesn't seem **fair** that I do more work than my co-workers.

    a. the same for all   **b.** correct   **c.** important

E ▸ WHAT DO YOU THINK?

Discuss your answers in a small group.

1. What are good ways to manage stress? Check the three best ideas.

   _____ Write down everything you have to do.

   _____ Plan ahead and do things early.

   _____ Talk about your problems with friends.

   _____ Do something fun (play the piano, read, see a movie).

   _____ Think about something happy.

   _____ Do physical activities (jogging, playing soccer).

   _____ Eat "comfort food" (foods that make you feel good, like ice
   cream or a special treat).

   _____ Get a lot of sleep.

   _____ (your idea)

2. What are the top three ways your classmates manage stress?

F ▸ READING FOR SPECIFIC INFORMATION

**This chart shows the most common ways that adults in the United States
manage stress. Read the chart and then answer the questions.**

Common Ways to Manage Stress	
Comfort eating	37%
Smoking	32%
Nail-biting	21%
Drinking alcohol	13%

1. The chart shows some unhealthy ways to manage stress. What are the
   two most common ways? Why are these unhealthy?

2. Are these similar or different from your ideas in exercise E above?

VOCABULARY REVIEW

A MATCHING

Match each word to the word or phrase with a similar meaning.

_____ 1. physical   **a.** in addition to

_____ 2. mental   **b.** try to understand

_____ 3. hard   **c.** reason

_____ 4. yell   **d.** of the body

_____ 5. manage   **e.** problem

_____ 6. on top of   **f.** use a loud voice

_____ 7. trouble   **g.** of the mind

_____ 8. chore   **h.** take care of

_____ 9. figure out   **i.** difficult

_____ 10. cause   **j.** something that you need to do regularly

B SENTENCE COMPLETION

Complete the sentences with words from the box.

caused	expect	figure out	manage	step
chores	fair	grown-ups	project	worry

1. We're working on a special _____ in class this week.

2. Could you help me _____ the answer to this question?

3. I can't stay out late. My parents _____ me to be home by 9:00 every night.

4. I need to find a job soon. I _____ a lot about that because I need the money.

5. They have eight children. I don't know how they _____.

6. What do we need to do next? What is our next _____?

7. I can't wait until we are _____ and we can do what we want.

8. I don't want more coffee. I think it _____ my stomachache.

9. Everyone in my family has _____ to do—washing the dishes, cooking, washing the clothes, and so on. We work together.

10. It isn't _____. He works every weekend, and he doesn't make a lot of money.

C CROSSWORD

Complete the puzzle.

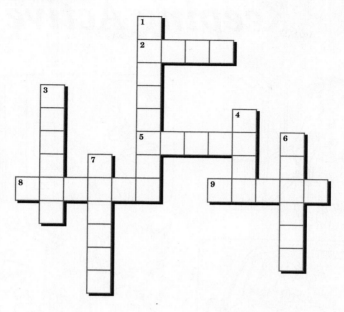

Across

2. difficult

5. make something happen

8. of the mind, not of the body

9. not with anyone else

Down

1. of the body, not of the mind

3. special work to do

4. speak very loudly

6. take care of

7. what you feel when you have a lot of things to do

Chapter 5 Keeping Active

a.

b.

c.

d.

e.

f.

g.

h.

A FIRST LOOK

A BACKGROUND BUILDING

Look at the pictures on page 62. Match the following sentences with the pictures. Then discuss the questions with a partner.

_____ I drive to work.   _____ I walk to work.

_____ I usually take the stairs.   _____ I usually take the elevator.

_____ I exercise every day.   _____ I usually watch TV for two hours a day.

_____ I work outside at least twice a week.   _____ I work on the computer about two hours a day.

1. How active are you? Underline the statements above that are true for you. Do you think that you get enough exercise?

2. Do you eat healthy food? How healthy is your diet? Rate your diet from 1 (not healthy) to 10 (very healthy).

1	2	3	4	5	6	7	8	9	10
(not healthy)									(very healthy)

3. Write six healthy foods that you like to eat.

_____   _____   _____

_____   _____   _____

4. Write six unhealthy foods that you like to eat.

_____   _____   _____

_____   _____   _____

Are We Active Enough?

1   Many people in the United States are active, but are they active enough? Doctors don't think so. Americans are getting fatter. Doctors say that 60 percent of American adults weigh too much and about 18 percent of these people are *obese.* This means they have too much body fat. When people are obese,   5 they are not healthy. They may have heart disease and other illnesses. They usually do not live as long as other people.

2   There are two main reasons people are obese. The first is diet. People eat too much, and too much of the food is unhealthy. The second is inactivity. People are not as active   10 today as they used to be. They don't exercise. They don't walk places. They watch more TV and spend more time in front of computers.

3   The problem is not just for adults. Doctors say that one in five children is overweight or obese. Children also eat too   15 much and are not as active as they used to be. There is a 20 percent chance that an obese child will grow up to be an obese adult.

4   So, what is the answer? We need to change our lifestyle, the way we live. Of course, people need to eat less and make   20 sure that the food they eat is healthy. People also need to become more active.

5   Doctors say that exercise is very important. People need to exercise at least three times a week for thirty minutes. When people are active, they stay healthy. Active people also live   25 longer. But many people say that they just don't have the time. They're just too busy.

C TOPIC

Read the topics below. Match each topic to a paragraph in the reading. Write the number of the paragraph on the line.

_____ many children eat too much

_____ exercise is important

_____ why more people are obese now

_____ Americans are getting fatter

_____ ways to change the situation

D VOCABULARY

Look back at the reading to find these words. The line number is in parentheses ( ). Then circle the letter of the word or phrase with a similar meaning.

1. enough (2)
   - **a.** at the right time
   - **b.** the right amount

2. disease (6)
   - **a.** medicine
   - **b.** illness

3. diet (9)
   - **a.** what we eat
   - **b.** how much we eat

4. unhealthy (10)
   - **a.** good for your body
   - **b.** not good for your body

5. inactivity (10)
   - **a.** moving around
   - **b.** not moving around

6. exercise (11)
   - **a.** get physical activity
   - **b.** go to sports events

7. overweight (15)

    a. weighing too much   **b.** working too hard

8. chance (17)

    a. possibility   **b.** time

E ▸ READING COMPREHENSION

Find the answers to the questions in the reading. Underline the answer and write the number of the question next to it.

1. How many adults in the United States weigh too much?

2. What does *obese* mean?

3. What problems can obese people have?

4. What are two reasons people are obese?

5. What are four reasons people are not as active as they used to be?

6. How many children in the United States are overweight or obese?

7. What percentage of obese children become obese adults?

8. How much time do people need to exercise each week?

A VOCABULARY

Complete the paragraph with words from the box.

active	doctors	healthy	overweight
diets	exercise	inactivity	weigh

In the United States, about 20 percent of children are

_____, and many of these children are obese. But obesity is

1

not just a problem in the United States. An organization called the

International Obesity Task Force says that obesity is a problem in other

places, too. In Europe, 20 percent of children between 5 and 17 years old

_____ too much. In China, this is true for 10 percent of

2

children. One reason is that children eat _____ full of high-

3

fat foods. Another reason is _____. _____ are

4   5

telling parents that their children need to be more _____.

6

They need to _____ more and eat _____ foods.

7   8

Read the following sentences carefully. Write T (true) or F (false).

_____ **1.** Doctors think people in the United States need to be more active.

_____ **2.** Everyone who is overweight is obese.

_____ **3.** Obesity is a cause of poor health.

_____ **4.** Obese people have shorter lives than people who are not obese.

_____ **5.** *Diet* means "what we eat."

_____ **6.** Two reasons for obesity are diet and inactivity.

_____ **7.** People who are not active live longer.

_____ **8.** Doctors say that people need to exercise every day.

C WHAT DO YOU THINK?

Discuss the questions in a small group.

1. Everyone knows that it's important to exercise. Why don't more people exercise?

2. Why do you think that children are less active today?

3. Obesity is not just a problem in the United States. Do you know anything about the problem in other countries?

 A BACKGROUND BUILDING

Look at the picture and discuss the questions in a small group.

1. Where is this boy?

2. What is he doing?

3. Is there any problem with this situation?

Here is one person's point of view. Read the story.

I teach fourth grade. In my school a lot of the students are overweight. Three students in my class are on diets. They're trying to lose weight, but it's very difficult to do. I feel sorry for them. It's not their fault that they're overweight. It's our fault.

We need to teach our children to eat healthy food. But look around you. Do parents eat healthy food? Do we cook healthy food? No. We eat at fast-food restaurants where the food isn't very healthy. Even at home, we don't cook fresh, healthy meals. We don't have the time.

In our schools, do we offer our kids healthy food? No. We give them pizza and chips at lunch. We sell them candy and soda. And only 30 percent of our schools have physical education classes. Our kids don't learn how to exercise and play games.

And then there's TV. Most children in the United States spend more than two hours a day after school watching TV. They are watching TV instead of playing outside. And while they watch TV, most kids eat snacks. They see ads on TV for unhealthy foods. They think, "If it's on TV, it's good for you."

No child should have to go on a diet. They should be able to eat healthy food, and we adults should make it easy for them to do that!

C TRUE OR FALSE?

Read the following sentences carefully. Write T (true) or F (false).

_____ 1. The writer teaches children.

_____ 2. Only three children in her school need to lose weight.

_____ 3. The writer thinks it's easy to lose weight.

_____ 4. The writer thinks the children are overweight because of adults.

_____ 5. The writer thinks that fast-food restaurants offer children healthy choices.

_____ 6. Most schools have classes in physical education.

_____ 7. The writer thinks that TV teaches children to make unhealthy food choices.

_____ 8. The writer thinks that it's good for children to watch TV.

D VOCABULARY

Circle the letter of the word or phrase closest in meaning to the boldfaced word(s) in the sentence.

1. I'm **on a diet**. I want to be healthy.
   a. on a special food plan   b. taking special medicine from the doctor

2. I want to **lose weight**.
   a. weigh more   b. weigh less

3. She looks very sad. I **feel sorry** for her.
   a. feel sad   b. feel angry

4. I like **fast food**, but most of it is unhealthy.
   a. fruits and vegetables   b. hamburgers and french fries

5. She **offered** the children apples and cheese.

   a. gave   **b.** made

6. I'm not very hungry. I had a **snack** a little earlier.

   a. small meal   **b.** dinner

7. The company put an **ad** in the newspaper.

   a. address   **b.** advertisement

8. **It is my fault** that we came late. I was finishing a project, so we left home late.

   a. It is because of me   **b.** It is my idea

 E ▶ **READING FOR SPECIFIC INFORMATION**

Read the chart and then answer the questions in a small group.

Overweight Children (ages 6–11) and Adolescents (ages 12–19)

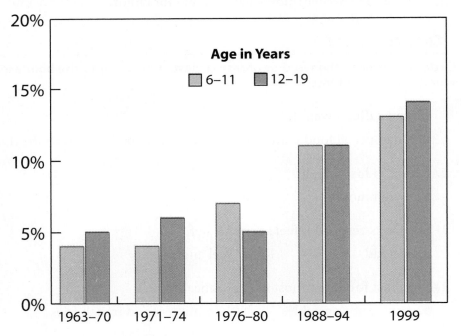

SOURCE: CDC/NCHS, NHES, and NHANES.

1. What does this chart show? Is it good news or bad news?

2. In the first period (1963 to 1970), what percent of adolescents were overweight?

3. In 1999, what percent of adolescents were overweight?

4. What percent of children were overweight during 1988–1994?

5. Was there a higher or lower percentage of overweight children in 1999 than during 1988–1994?

F ▶ WHAT DO YOU THINK?

Discuss the questions in a small group.

1. Some people think the government should help solve the problem of childhood obesity. What do you think about these ideas?

   a. The government should put a tax (extra money) on unhealthy foods. Then it should use the money to teach people how to cook healthy foods.

   b. Food companies should not advertise unhealthy food to children on TV.

   c. Schools should not sell soda or unhealthy snacks.

2. What other ideas can you think of to solve the problem of overweight children?

VOCABULARY REVIEW

A MATCHING

Match each word to the word or phrase with a similar meaning.

_____ 1. inactivity   **a.** not moving around

_____ 2. lose weight   **b.** give

_____ 3. disease   **c.** the right amount

_____ 4. offer   **d.** weigh less

_____ 5. snack   **e.** small meal

_____ 6. healthy   **f.** feel sad

_____ 7. feel sorry   **g.** illness

_____ 8. enough   **h.** good for you

B SENTENCE COMPLETION

Complete the sentences with words from the box.

active	fault	offered	sorry
ad	healthy	snack	weight

1. I know fast food isn't as _____ as fresh food, but I'm very busy. I usually eat out at least three times a week.

2. People use their free time in lots of ways. Some like to be physically _____.

3. She's trying to lose _____, but it's very difficult. I feel _____ for her.

4. I saw the _____ for the car in the newspaper.

5. I was driving home from work and stopped at a stop sign. Another driver ran into the back of my car. It was his _____.

6. She _____ me coffee, but I don't drink coffee. I said, "No thanks."

7. I don't eat too much at breakfast or lunch, but in the afternoon I eat a(n) _____ . Then, sometimes, I don't feel like eating dinner.

C CROSSWORD

Complete the puzzle.

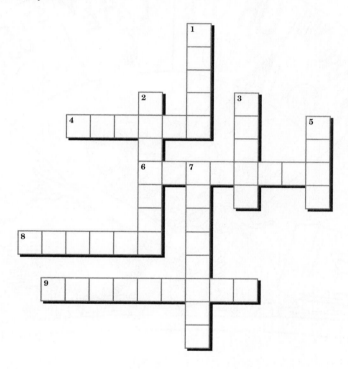

Across

4. the opposite of *inactive*
6. do physical activity
8. possibility
9. the opposite of *healthy*

Down

1. very overweight
2. illness
3. "Every night I _____ TV."
5. special food plan
7. It's faster than the stairs.

Chapter **6** On Schedule

A BACKGROUND BUILDING

Work with a partner. Discuss these questions.

1. Look at the picture on page 76. Why is the woman unhappy?

2. Is your schedule very busy, or do you have some free time?

3. Do you manage your time well? Look at the ideas below. Put a check next to the things you do.

_____ Spend ten to fifteen minutes planning your day.

_____ Make a "to-do" list. (things you need to do)

_____ First, do the difficult things on your list. Then do the easy things.

_____ Always carry an appointment book with you and use it.

_____ Do things during your lunchtime.

_____ Make time to be with family and friends.

_____ Spend some time relaxing or exercising every day. This will give you more energy to manage your time.

4. Do you have other ideas to manage your time?

Families on the Run

1   Everyone is "on the run" now. Even children are too busy. They go to school during the day. Then they go to an after-school program if their parents work. After school or on weekends, they often go to dance class, swimming lessons, and soccer practice. Dinner is on the run, at a fast-food   5
restaurant or even in the car.

2   Things used to be different. Young children learned to swim in the summer. They didn't take swimming lessons after school. They played sports outside with their neighborhood friends. Baseball practice was once a week, not two or three   10
times. The family ate dinner together at home every evening.

3   Why is everyone so busy now? There are many reasons. First, parents want their children to learn how to do things. They want their children to learn skills that they will need when they get older. "Will my child be a famous artist? Then she   15
needs art lessons now!" thinks the mother of a 5-year-old. "My child needs to learn about winning and losing. Team sports are important," thinks the father of a 7-year-old. Parents are also worried because *other* children may know more than their own children. They don't want their children to fall behind. They   20
want to be good parents.

4   Some parents are trying to slow down. They started a group called Putting Family First. Here are some of their ideas:

- Have dinner together as a family. Family time is more important than lessons.   25
- Do not make your child's schedule too busy.

• Make sure that your children can miss lessons and games for family activities.
• Make sure that teams do not have activities on holidays.

5   It's hard for parents and children to cut back on activities.   30 But sometimes children should just play and have fun.

C TOPIC

Read the topics below. Match each topic to a paragraph in the reading. Write the number of the paragraph on the line.

_____ how to slow down

_____ reasons families are busy now

_____ people are busy now

_____ things were different in the past

_____ children need to cut back and have fun

D VOCABULARY

Look back at the reading to find these words. The line number is in parentheses ( ). Then circle the letter of the word or phrase with a similar meaning.

1. on the run (1)
   a. fast
   b. in a hurry

2. together (11)
   a. in common with
   b. with other people

3. reasons (12)
   a. why things happen
   b. when things happen

4. winning (17)
   a. being first
   b. being last

5. losing (17)

    a. being first   **b.** not being first

6. slow down (22)

    a. stop   **b.** not go so fast

7. schedule (26)

    a. free time   **b.** plan

8. miss (27)

    a. not go to   **b.** go to

9. holidays (29)

    a. weekdays   **b.** special days

10. cut back on (30)

    a. not do as many   **b.** be busy

E READING COMPREHENSION

Answer the questions about the reading.

1. Why are children so busy now? Check the answers that are in the reading.

_____ The schoolday is longer now.

_____ Many parents work, so children go to after-school programs.

_____ After-school lessons and sports are popular now.

_____ Dinner is not so important nowadays.

_____ Parents want their children to learn new skills.

_____ Parents want their children to know what other children know.

2. Do these sentences describe things that are happening now or in the past? Write *Now* or *Past* on the line.

_____ Families often eat dinner at fast-food restaurants.

_____ Families eat dinner together at home.

_____ Children take swimming lessons only in the summer.

_____ Children play sports in the neighborhood.

_____ Athletic teams practice once a week.

3. Check the suggestions that you think Putting Family First agrees with.

_____ Have baseball practice at dinnertime.

_____ Take your children to lessons three times a week.

_____ Do not join a team that plays games on Thanksgiving Day.

_____ The soccer coach says you can never miss a practice or game.

_____ The baseball coach says you can be absent twice every month.

_____ Make sure your child has free time at home.

LOOK AGAIN

A VOCABULARY

Complete the paragraph with words from the box.

cut back on	games	lessons	schedules	together
fall behind	hard	practice	skills	worried

My husband and I have two sons. When they were little, we always

had dinner _____. Right now, we almost never see each
                    1

other because our _____ are so busy. The boys have soccer
                        2

_____ two times a week (but on different nights), and on
        3

Saturdays they play their _____. They also take piano
                                4

_____ once a week. It's _____ to fit in their
        5   6

homework! I'm _____ that we're doing too much. I'd like
                    7

to _____ our activities, but it's not easy to do. My sons love
        8

sports and want to improve their _____, but I don't want
                                        9

them to _____ at school.
            10

B ▶ READING COMPREHENSION

Complete these sentences about "the old days" and "nowadays" from the reading.

1. In the old days, children learned to swim _____.
   Nowadays, they take _____.

2. In the old days, the family _____. Today, the
   family is often too busy _____.

3. In the old days, sports practice was _____.
   These days, practice is _____.

4. In the old days, children learned to play sports in their _____.
   Nowadays, they learn _____.

C ▶ WHAT DO YOU THINK?

Discuss the questions in a small group.

1. Why are things different for children now than in the past?

2. Do you think children are unhappy about their busy lives?

3. Do you think parents should cut back on children's activities?

4. When you were younger, how did you spend your time? Do you think
   you were too busy?

A POINT OF VIEW

A ▸ BACKGROUND BUILDING

Discuss the questions in a small group.

1. What time does this teenager have to get up? What time does he go to bed?

2. Is he a morning person (someone who likes to wake up early) or a night person (someone who works best at night)? How do you know?

3. Are you a morning person or a night person? Why?

Here is one person's point of view. Read the story.

I can't get up in the morning. I don't even hear my alarm clock when it rings at 6:30. My mother has to shake me to wake me up.

I think 6:30 is much too early for anyone to be up. I just can't get enough sleep. I am always tired. I'm a night person, and I stay up late at night. I have lots of energy at 10:00 or 11:00 at night. But when the morning comes, I can't get up.

My first class starts at 7:30, and I rush to get there. Well, my body is there, but my mind is still asleep. I don't understand why we have to start school so early. None of my friends are ready to study math or chemistry when they are still half asleep.

Scientists who study teenagers know that they need a lot of sleep. They know that teenagers usually don't do well in the morning. I don't understand why we don't start school at 9:00. Most businesses open at 9:00 or even 10:00 a.m. Who had the idea to begin the schoolday so early? I'm sure it was a morning person, not a night person—and not a teenager, either.

C ▶ TRUE OR FALSE?

Read the following sentences carefully. Write T (true) or F (false).

_____ 1. The writer is a teenager.

_____ 2. The writer is a morning person.

_____ 3. The writer is ready to do things at night.

_____ 4. The alarm clock wakes the writer up.

_____ 5. The writer's school starts at 8:30 A.M.

_____ 6. The writer has a job.

_____ 7. Scientists say that teenagers don't need much sleep.

_____ 8. The writer thinks the early school schedule is a terrible idea.

D ▶ VOCABULARY

Find the word(s) in the reading that match the definition. The paragraph number is in parentheses ( ). Write the word(s) on the line.

1. stop sleeping (1)   _____

2. move someone or something quickly (1)   _____

3. sleepy (2)   _____

4. the opposite of _go slowly_ (3)   _____

5. the opposite of _late_ (3)   _____

6. the opposite of _all_ (3)   _____

7. the opposite of _awake_ (3)   _____

8. begin (4)   _____

E WHAT DO YOU THINK?

Discuss the questions in a small group.

1. Do you think teenagers need more sleep than older (or younger) people?

2. Should teenagers have a special schedule (start school later)?

F READING FOR SPECIFIC INFORMATION

Read the article. Then complete the chart.

Why do teenagers have such a hard time waking up in the morning? High school and college students need more sleep than children or adults. They need almost ten hours per night.

Younger children need only about nine hours of sleep. Most adults seem to get even fewer hours. Seven to eight hours is the average number of hours of sleep for adults.

Teenagers need more sleep because their bodies are growing and changing. Their brains are also changing. They have more to do in the evening and go to bed late. Going to bed late makes it hard to get up the next day.

Some high schools are changing their schedules. They are starting later in the morning so that teenagers are in school in both body and mind.

Who Needs More Sleep?	
Who?	**How many hours of sleep do they need?**
	9 hours
Teenagers	
Adults	

VOCABULARY REVIEW

A MATCHING

Match each word to the word or phrase with a similar meaning.

_____ 1. reason   **a.** time plan

_____ 2. worried   **b.** not go so fast

_____ 3. start   **c.** not do so much

_____ 4. slow down   **d.** in a hurry

_____ 5. winning   **e.** difficult

_____ 6. cut back on   **f.** not go to

_____ 7. on the run   **g.** why something happens

_____ 8. miss   **h.** being first

_____ 9. hard   **i.** begin

_____ 10. schedule   **j.** you feel this way when you have a lot to do

B SENTENCE COMPLETION

Complete the sentences with words from the box.

asleep	early	missed	reason
cut back on	famous	practice	worried

1. If you play football, there is _____ three times a week.

2. He stays up late at night. That's the _____ he is always tired in class.

3. If you telephoned at 6:30 this morning, I didn't hear it. I was still

_____ .

4. I think 6:30 in the morning is too _____ to call someone.

5. If you're too busy, why don't you _____ some of your activities?

6. I was sick last week, so I _____ class twice.

7. I'm _____ about my father. I think he's working too hard.

8. Everyone knows her name. She's _____.

C CROSSWORD

Complete the puzzle.

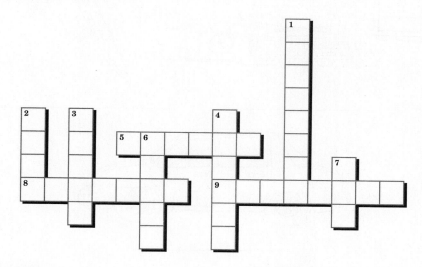

Across

5. the opposite of awake
8. special day
9. the plan for your time

Down

1. time when you do something to get better at it
2. hurry
3. the opposite of *late*
4. why something happens
6. begin
7. on the _____ (very busy)

Chapter 7 Inventions

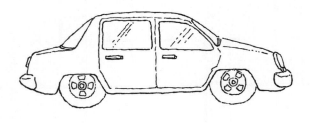

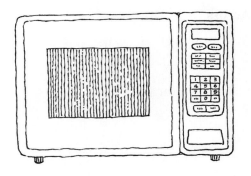

| car | cell phone | computer | microwave oven | toothbrush |

A FIRST LOOK

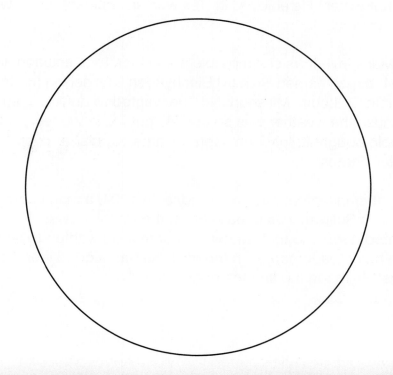 A BACKGROUND BUILDING

Work with a partner. Discuss these questions.

1. Match the inventions to the pictures on page 90. Write the name of the invention under the picture.

2. Which of these five inventions is the most important for your life? Choose only one.

3. Which inventions did the other students in the class choose? Count up the totals.

4. Change the totals into percentages. For example, four students in a class of ten = 4/10 = 40 percent; three students in a class of twenty-two = 3/22 = 14 percent. Which invention is most popular in your class or group?

5. Using these percentages, complete the pie chart for your class.

Inventions or Accidents?

1   Look around you right now and you will see a number of inventions. Maybe you are sitting at a desk, and you are using a lamp. You are reading this book and using a pencil or pen. These inventions and many others make our lives easier and better. But where did these things come from? Who invented   5 them? And why?

2   Many inventions happened by accident the first time. Tea is a good example. Here is the story: In China, almost 5,000 years ago, Shen Nong, a Chinese leader, told the people to boil their water. He knew that this made the water safe to drink.   10 One day, someone was boiling water. The leaves from a nearby plant fell into the water. It smelled good, so Shen Nong tasted the hot water. He enjoyed it! Tea was an accident, but it was here to stay!

3   Many inventors see a problem and look for a solution. In   15 1904, a man named Richard Blechynden was selling hot tea at a fair in St. Louis, Missouri. No one wanted to drink his tea because the weather was so hot. He put ice in the tea, and people bought it. Iced tea soon became popular all over the United States.   20

4   Other inventors have a new idea. In 1904, a man named Thomas Sullivan was a tea seller in the United States. He wanted people to try his new kind of tea. He wanted to send a little bit of tea to people in the mail. He had a good idea—tea bags! He made the first tea bags from silk.   25

5   Sullivan thought people would cut open the bags and use the tea, but many people made the tea by putting the whole tea bag in the water. This was easy, and it was also easy to wash the cup. His customers helped to invent the tea bag because they figured out the best way to use it to prepare tea. 30

6   Even average people can be inventors!

C TOPIC

Read the topics below. Match each topic to a paragraph in the reading. Write the number of the paragraph on the line.

_____ finding a solution to a problem

_____ inventions all around us

_____ people used Sullivan's idea in a different way

_____ inventions happen by accident

_____ a new idea to sell something

D VOCABULARY

Look back at the reading to find these words. The line number is in parentheses ( ). Then circle the letter of the word or phrase with a similar meaning.

1. a number of (1)
   a. many   **b.** not many

2. by accident (7)
   a. planned ahead   **b.** not planned

3. boil (9)
   a. drink   **b.** heat

4. safe (10)
   a. healthy   **b.** easy

5. fell (12)

    a. became hot   **b.** dropped

6. tasted (12)

    a. tried   **b.** finished

7. solution (15)

    a. answer   **b.** problem

8. fair (17)

    a. event   **b.** kind

9. prepare (30)

    a. make   **b.** enjoy

10. average (31)

    a. special   **b.** usual

E ▸ READING COMPREHENSION

Find the answers to the questions in the reading. Underline the answer and write the number of the question next to it.

1. What are three examples of inventions in the first paragraph?

2. Why did the Chinese leader tell people to boil water?

3. How did the Chinese make tea the first time?

4. Why did Richard Blechynden get the idea to make iced tea?

5. When Thomas Sullivan sent tea in small bags, what did he think people would do? What really happened?

LOOK AGAIN

A VOCABULARY

Complete the paragraph with words from the box.

all over	boil	hot	leaves	stay
bag	happened	iced	popular	taste

Tea is the most _____ 1 drink in the world after water.

People _____ 2 the world drink tea. People usually drink

_____ 3 tea. They _____ 4 water and then they

add tea _____ 5 or a tea _____ 6 with tea inside

to the water. The tea has to _____ 7 in the tea pot or in the

cup for a while to _____ 8 good. In the United States, people

like _____ 9 tea as well as hot tea. It depends on the weather.

What a delicious drink, and just think—it _____ 10 by

accident.

B READING COMPREHENSION

Circle the letter of the answer that best completes each sentence. Look back at the reading to find the answers.

1. According to the first paragraph, you will see inventions ____.
   - **a.** in a few places
   - **b.** wherever you are

2. The writer tells the story of tea because it happened ____.
   - **a.** a long time ago
   - **b.** by accident

3. The Chinese leader said that everyone _____ boil water.

   a. wanted to   **b.** needed to

4. People boiled water because _____.

   a. it tasted good   **b.** it was healthy

5. Tea happened for the first time when tea leaves fell _____.

   a. into boiling water   **b.** to the ground

6. Richard Blechynden was the first person to sell _____.

   a. tea   **b.** iced tea

7. The reading says that iced tea is popular _____.

   a. everywhere   **b.** in the U.S.

8. Thomas Sullivan sent tea to people so that they _____.

   a. could try it   **b.** could sell it

9. Thomas Sullivan _____ that people would boil the whole bag.

   a. knew   **b.** was surprised

10. Tea bags became popular because they were _____.

   a. easy to use   **b.** inexpensive

 ## C ▶ READING FOR SPECIFIC INFORMATION

Look again on page 91. Then read the article and fill in the chart that follows with information from the survey.

> Researchers in Boston, Massachusetts wanted to know the answer to this question: Which of these five inventions do you need in your life? The choices were a microwave oven, a cell phone, a computer, a car, or a toothbrush. They asked two groups: one was a group of 400 teenagers; the other was a group of 1,000 adults.

Here are the results:

- The toothbrush was the first choice for both the teenagers and the adults. Forty-two percent of the adults and thirty-four percent of the teenagers chose a toothbrush.

- The second choice was the car. Thirty-one percent of the teenagers and thirty-seven percent of the adults said the car was most important to them.

- Six percent of the adults and sixteen percent of the teenagers said a computer was most important.

- Six percent of the adults chose the cell phone and another six percent chose the microwave.

- Ten percent of the teenagers chose the cell phone.

- Seven percent of the teenagers chose the microwave.

	Percentage of Adults	Percentage of Teenagers
A microwave oven		
A cell phone		
A computer		
A car		
A toothbrush		

Discuss the questions in a small group.

1. How did the percentages in the survey on page 97 compare to your class's choices? Were your choices different? Can you explain why?

2. The survey asked about only five inventions. With your classmates, make a list of other inventions important to your life.

3. Now make a list of the inventions that you see around you. What do you know about these inventions? Did they happen by accident? Were they solutions to a problem? Choose one invention and use the Internet to research where it came from.

4. What invention is most important for you in your own life?

A POINT OF VIEW

A BACKGROUND BUILDING

Discuss the questions in a small group.

1. What is the woman in the picture doing?

2. How does she feel? Why?

B READING

Here is one person's point of view. Read the story.

It's hard to keep up with all the new things we use to communicate with each other! We're always in touch with other people. My co-workers call my cell phone day and night, weekdays and weekends. They also e-mail me night and day. They send me information about projects at work all the time.

We can't escape from work. Last summer I finally took a vacation. I saw a woman answering her e-mail at the beach!

It's great that it is so easy to keep in touch with other people. But it's not great that we're in touch all the time. A woman I know has a solution. She uses e-mail at work every day, but she does not have e-mail at home. She keeps her work at work and her private life at home.

I thought that inventions like e-mail and cell phones would make our lives easier and better. But I think they just mean more work.

C TRUE OR FALSE?

Read the following sentences carefully. Write T (true) or F (false).

_____ **1.** The writer thinks that inventions make staying in touch easier.

_____ **2.** The writer doesn't want to communicate with other people.

_____ **3.** The writer uses e-mail and a cell phone.

_____ **4.** People from work call the writer at night.

_____ **5.** Co-workers call the writer all the time.

_____ **6.** The writer thinks that it is easy to get away from work.

_____ **7.** The writer thinks that it is a bad idea to answer e-mail on the beach.

_____ 8. The writer likes to be in contact with co-workers all the time.

_____ 9. The woman who works with the writer doesn't use e-mail.

_____ 10. The writer thinks inventions make work easier.

D VOCABULARY

Circle the letter of the word or phrase closest in meaning to the boldfaced word(s) in the sentence.

1. I can't **keep up with** my e-mail.
   a. manage   **b.** find out about   **c.** understand

2. I don't use e-mail much. I like to **communicate** on the telephone.
   a. work   **b.** share information   **c.** understand

3. My sister and I **are in touch** once a week.
   a. visit   **b.** are friendly   **c.** speak or write

4. The cat was trying to **escape** from the dog. It climbed up the tree.
   a. return   **b.** take   **c.** get away

5. She **answers** her e-mail in the morning.
   a. reads   **b.** sends answers to   **c.** looks for

6. Last year I went to Brazil on **vacation**.
   a. time away from work   **b.** weekends   **c.** a schedule

7. I don't know how they found out my **private** information. I didn't want them to know.
   a. not for everyone   **b.** important   **c.** expensive

8. Some inventions **mean** a change in how we do things.
   a. expect   **b.** cause   **c.** show

E **WHAT DO YOU THINK?**

Discuss the questions in a small group.

1. How do you communicate? Do you write letters? Do you use a cell phone? Do you use e-mail?

2. Do you stay in touch in different ways with your friends? Your co-workers? Your classmates? Your family?

3. What do you think is the most important invention for communication?

4. Think of a new invention. What is something we need in our lives?

VOCABULARY REVIEW

 A **MATCHING**

Match each word to the word or phrase with a similar meaning.

_____	1. bag	**a.** not a question
_____	2. answer	**b.** usual
_____	3. a number of	**c.** the opposite of *cold*
_____	4. be in touch	**d.** this can hold things
_____	5. hot	**e.** speak or write to someone
_____	6. private	**f.** for yourself or your family, not for everyone
_____	7. communicate	**g.** many
_____	8. average	**h.** share information

B SENTENCE COMPLETION

Complete the sentences with words from the box.

accident	escape	ice	leaves	solution
are in touch	happened	keep up with	mean	taste

1. It was a quiet day. Nothing _____.
2. I don't live near my family, but we _____ with each other.
3. Tea wasn't an invention. It was a(n) _____.
4. It's hard to _____ from work when you own a business.
5. The green parts of a plant are _____.
6. If you leave that _____ in the car, it will turn into water in fifteen minutes.
7. This is a big problem. We'll have to try to find a(n) _____.
8. What do you _____? I don't understand.
9. The tea leaves in the hot water made the water _____ good.
10. Everyone in the family is very busy. It's hard to _____ all the activities.

C CROSSWORD

Complete the puzzle.

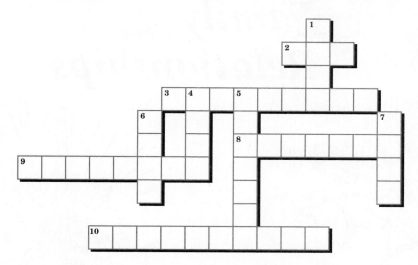

Across

2. you drive this

3. people read e-mail on their _____

8. make, get something ready

9. time away from work

10. you use this to clean your teeth

Down

1. When you boil water, it is _____ to drink.

4. you bake things in this

5. liked by a lot of people

6. heat water to a high temperature

7. a type of phone

Chapter 8 Family Relationships

1. _____

_____

2. _____

_____

3. _____

_____

A FIRST LOOK

A BACKGROUND BUILDING

Work with a partner. Discuss these questions.

1. Read the words. Which ones describe you?

    _____ a leader

    _____ friendly

    _____ talks a lot

    _____ intelligent

    _____ shy

    _____ funny

    _____ wants to be perfect

2. Each child in a family has a different personality. Also, the oldest child in a family is usually different from a middle child or the youngest child. Are you the oldest, youngest, or in the middle in your family?

3. Which words above do you think describe an oldest child, a middle child, and a youngest child?

4. Look at the pictures of the salesperson, the businessperson, and the soccer player on page 104. Match the jobs to the pictures on page 104. Write the name of the job under the picture.

5. Which jobs would you expect an oldest child to have? A middle child? A youngest child? Write *oldest, middle,* and *youngest* under the pictures. Discuss your choices.

Family Relationships

1   Psychologists study people. They want to know why people are the way they are. They often study family relationships. The relationship with our parents is important. So are the relationships with our brothers and sisters. These relationships make us who we are.   5

2   Some psychologists also think that our birth order is very important. Birth order is where you are in your family, your position. Are you the oldest? Are you the youngest? Or are you in the middle? Children in different positions have different personalities.   10

3   Oldest, or first-born, children are willing to work hard. They take care of other people and are responsible at their jobs. Many first-born children want to be perfect. They pay attention to everything, even small details. They are often leaders, the people in control. A child without brothers and sisters, an   15 *only child*, is similar to a first-born child.

4   Middle children get along well with other people, and they like to help solve problems. They are sometimes shy, but they have many friends.

5   Youngest, or last-born, children in the family are often very   20 friendly and funny. They talk a lot and love being around other people.

6   Of course, there are many things that shape a person's personality. Birth order is only one thing. But it may help to explain a person's personality.   25

C TOPIC

Read the topics below. Match each topic to a paragraph in the reading. Write the number of the paragraph on the line.

_____ description of youngest children

_____ birth order is important

_____ birth order is one way to understand people better

_____ description of middle children

_____ description of first-borns

_____ psychologists study family relationships

D VOCABULARY

Find the word(s) in the reading that match the definition. The line number is in parentheses ( ). Write the word(s) on the line.

1. scientists who study people (1)   _____

2. the connection people have with each other (3) _____

3. exactly right (13)   _____

4. watch or listen to carefully (13)   _____

5. single pieces of information (14)   _____

6. the people in control (14)   _____

7. someone with no brothers or sisters (16)   _____

8. quiet, doesn't talk much (18)   _____

9. being near, spending time with (21)   _____

10. make a certain way (23)   _____

Find the answers to the questions in the reading. Underline the answer and write the number of the question next to it.

1. Why do psychologists study people?

2. What family relationships are important?

3. What does *birth order* mean?

4. What are oldest children often like?

5. What are youngest children often like?

6. What are middle children often like?

LOOK AGAIN

A ► **VOCABULARY**

Complete the sentences with words from the box.

details	pay attention to	position	responsible	solved
gets along with	personality	relationship	shy	willing to

1. She is always nice. She _____ everyone.

2. When he reads, he remembers all the _____: the dates, the years, the time, and the names of all the people. I usually only remember the main idea.

3. She has a good _____ with her boss. They work well together.

4. I don't know how to make bread, but I'm _____ try. Can you show me?

5. My car wasn't working, but the mechanic _____ the problem.

6. My sister doesn't like to talk in class. She's very _____.

7. What is your _____ in your family—are you the first-born?

8. Everyone is talking. It's hard to _____ the teacher.

9. How would you describe your _____? Are you quiet or do you talk a lot?

10. Which person in your family takes care of everyone else—who is the most _____?

B READING COMPREHENSION

According to the reading, which child probably does these things? Write oldest, middle, and/or youngest on the line.

1. tell jokes: _____

2. take a friend to the doctor: _____

3. not talk a lot: _____

4. work on something to make it perfect: _____

5. always get good grades at school: _____

6. try to make someone feel better: _____

7. talk a lot: _____

8. take care of other people in the family: _____

9. make new friends easily: _____

10. not take vacations often: _____

C READING FOR SPECIFIC INFORMATION

Decide which jobs go with which family position. Write 1 (oldest or only child), 2 (middle child), or 3 (youngest) on the line.

_____ 1. writer

_____ 2. astronaut

_____ 3. manager

_____ 4. comedian

_____ 5. doctor

_____ 6. professional athlete

_____ 7. president

_____ 8. diplomat or lawyer

_____ 9. salesperson

_____ 10. college professor

Now read the information about job choices and check your answers.

First-born children (and only children) often choose high-status jobs. Parents give their first-born children a lot of attention, and they expect a lot from them. Parents want them to have important jobs, and they often do.

First-borns are usually leaders. Many presidents of the United States were first-born children. First-borns are also willing to try new things. Many astronauts are first-borns. Many doctors and college professors are also first-born children.

Children in the middle usually want to be different from the first-born. They are good at listening to different opinions and solving problems. They are often diplomats or lawyers. They are also good with groups of people. They are often managers or members of a team. Some middle children become professional athletes.

The last-born, the "baby" of the family, is often friendly. Last-borns like to talk a lot and often choose jobs as salespeople. They also like humor and are good at telling stories. They sometimes become comedians (people who tell funny jokes or stories) or writers.

D ▶ WHAT DO YOU THINK?

Discuss the questions in a small group.

1. Divide into groups by birth order. In your groups, talk about the descriptions of birth-order personalities. Are they true for each group?

2. Make a list of your brothers, sisters, and other people you know. Next to each name, write the person's birth order (*first, middle,* or *last*). Then write that person's job. Do the jobs match the personalities according to birth order? Share your lists with your group.

3. As a class, discuss the question: Do you agree or disagree with the psychologists about birth order? Why or why not?

A POINT OF VIEW

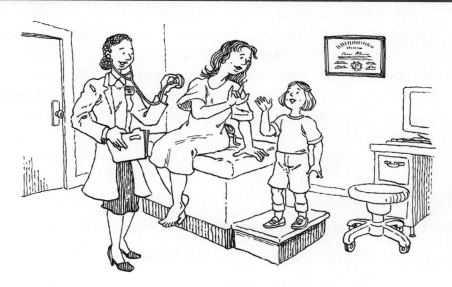

A ▶ BACKGROUND BUILDING

Discuss the questions in a small group.

1. In your family, who helps other family members? Who takes care of the youngest and oldest people? Do you help or take care of anyone in your family?

2. Who are the people in the picture? What are they doing?

B ▶ READING

Here is one person's point of view. Read the story.

It is not easy being the oldest in the family. Sometimes I think I was never a child. I remember that my parents took care of me when I was very young. Then, before I even began school, I started to take care of them. I was the oldest, and I had to be responsible. This is because they are deaf and I'm not. I can hear. Even as a young child, I was their ears and voice. They took me to school, but I talked to the teachers for them. I missed school when they were ill because I had to go to the doctor with them. I quickly became the parent in our family.

My parents don't expect so much from my brother and sister. They aren't much help. We all live near my parents. But who do my parents call? Me. Who knows when they have to go to the doctor? I do. I often ask my brother and sister to do things, but then they call and ask me a lot of questions. Sometimes they don't do things the right way. It's usually easier to do everything myself. Why is it always my responsibility?

C ▶ TRUE OR FALSE?

Read the following sentences carefully. Write T (true) or F (false).

_____   1. The writer is the oldest in the family.

_____   2. The writer has two sisters.

_____   3. The writer feels responsible for her parents.

_____   4. The writer is deaf.

_____   5. The writer spends a lot of time helping her parents.

_____   6. The writer's parents expect her brother and sister to help them.

_____ 7. The writer's brother and sister live with their parents.

_____ 8. It's less trouble for the writer to do things herself.

D VOCABULARY

Complete the paragraph with words from the box.

calls	expects	responsibility	takes care of
deaf	ill	right	voice

In every family, there is usually one person who _____
                                                        1
everyone. It's usually the father or mother, but in some families parents

need children to take care of them. For example, if a parent is

_____ and can't hear, the child may take
        2

_____ for the family. When the parent is
        3

_____, the child goes along to the doctor. When someone
        4

_____ on the telephone, the child answers. The child
        5

becomes the parent's _____ because he or she is the one
                              6

everyone _____ to speak for the parents. Is it
                7

_____ for children to be the parents in the family?
        8

WHAT DO YOU THINK?

Discuss the questions in a small group.

1. How does the writer feel about taking care of her parents?

2. What things are difficult for people who are deaf?

3. The writer says, "I quickly became the parent." What does the writer mean?

4. Is there anything the writer can do to change this situation?

VOCABULARY REVIEW

A MATCHING

Match each word to the word or phrase with a similar meaning.

_____ 1. personality	**a.** exactly right
_____ 2. get along with	**b.** be near
_____ 3. solve	**c.** quiet, doesn't talk a lot
_____ 4. shy	**d.** have a good relationship with
_____ 5. call	**e.** not able to hear
_____ 6. deaf	**f.** telephone
_____ 7. be around	**g.** find an answer for
_____ 8. perfect	**h.** the way you are

Complete the paragraphs with words from the box.

details	ill	responsible	take care of
expect	position	solve	willing to

Mei Ling is very _____. She has four sisters. If one of
1

her sisters gets _____ at school, she goes to get her. She can
2

always _____ the family's problems.
3

Mei Ling is always _____ help her parents. They don't
4

speak English, so she speaks for them when they go to the doctor. At

home, she likes to _____ the little things, the
5

_____. Mei Ling's parents are very proud of her. They
6

_____ her to do great things when she is older.
7

What _____ in the family do you think Mei Ling has? Is
8

she the oldest, middle, or youngest child?

Complete the puzzle.

Across

4. you use this when you speak

6. they study people

8. someone with no brothers or sisters, an _____ child

Down

1. not oldest or youngest; in the _____

2. make something a certain way

3. correct, the way things should be

5. "Be careful! Pay _____."

7. "They argue a lot. They don't _____ along."

NOTES

NOTES